Discovering Greatness:

A Journey into American History

Faith Faye Henderson

Dedication

Dear young people Both boys and girls. You are the star of this book. know that Beyond any present pain, there is joy waiting for you in the future. As You are in the process of discovering yourselves and navigating your way through life's journeys,

May you find the beauty and greatness in every step along the way.

Enjoy this book dear _______ because it was written with so much love just for you.

About the Author

Faith Henderson was the last of five children born to her single mother in the 1970s. Faith lost her father to cancer in 1994, and since 2013, she has been her mother's primary caregiver. She became a single mother herself at fourteen years of age. She is well represented by her two children, Paris Henderson and Joseph Branch, who have given her four grandchildren to date—three grandsons and one granddaughter, to whom this book is dedicated.

Faith has worn many hats that have assisted in shaping who she is today: from sales associate, nursing assistant, entrepreneur, childcare provider, homeowner, multi-business owner, volunteer firefighter, and now published author, daughter, sister, mother, adoptive mother, grandmother, provider, nurturer, and motivator. Her beliefs are that children are our future, and it is our job to protect, love, and teach them out loud, aiding them in becoming psychologically and emotionally strong, purposeful humans.

Contents

Chapter 1

Discovering Greatness

Discovering greatness is like finding hidden treasures in everyday moments. It's about realizing the extraordinary in the ordinary and the profound in the simple. Greatness isn't confined to grand gestures; it resides in small acts of kindness, the relentless pursuit of passion, and the resilience to overcome challenges. It's the quiet strength within, the unwavering belief that every effort, no matter how modest, contributes to a larger purpose. Greatness is not a destination but a journey, an exploration of one's potential. In simple words, it's the joy of uncovering the exceptional in the familiar, the magic in the mundane.

Concept of Greatness Within Oneself

At its core, greatness within oneself is the idea that each person possesses unique qualities and capabilities that, when recognized and nurtured, can lead to remarkable achievements and a fulfilling life. It's about tapping into one's potential, embracing strengths, and overcoming limitations. This concept encourages individuals to explore the depths of their character, talents, and aspirations to discover the greatness that resides within them.

Imagine greatness as a hidden treasure within you, waiting to be unearthed. Just like a seed carries the potential to grow into a mighty tree, every person carries the seeds of greatness within themselves. It's not about comparison or competition with others; it's a personal journey of self-discovery and self-realization.

To understand this concept, let's break it down into a few key aspects:

Recognizing Your Uniqueness

Greatness within oneself begins with recognizing your uniqueness. No two individuals are exactly alike, and that's the beauty of it. It's like being a piece of a jigsaw puzzle – you have a specific shape and place that fits without a glitch into the grand picture of life. This uniqueness is not just about external appearances but extends to your thoughts, emotions, and experiences. Embrace what makes you different, for it is often these differences that contribute to your greatness.

Embracing Your Strengths

Everyone has strengths – those things they excel at or feel passionate about. It could be a talent for problem-solving, a compassionate nature, or a creative mind. Recognizing and embracing your strengths is a crucial step toward unlocking your greatness. It's not about being perfect at everything but understanding where you shine the brightest. Your strengths are like tools in a toolbox, ready to be used to build the life you envision.

Overcoming Challenges

Life is full of challenges, big and small. Overcoming problems is an essential part of the journey towards greatness. Think of challenges as stepping stones that help you grow and evolve. The way you navigate through difficulties, learn from setbacks, and persist in the face of adversity defines your greatness. It's about resilience and the ability to turn challenges into opportunities for personal development.

Pursuing Passions

Passions are like guiding stars that lead you toward your greatness. What is it that makes your heart beat faster?

What actions bring you immense joy and satisfaction? Identifying and pursuing your passions is a key aspect of unlocking the greatness within. It could be anything – from artistic endeavors to scientific pursuits. When you are involved in actions that align with your passions, you not only enjoy the process but also uncover hidden potentials within yourself.

Contributing to Something Bigger

Greatness within oneself extends beyond personal achievements; it involves contributing positively to the world around you. It's about recognizing that your actions, no matter how small, have an impact on the larger tapestry of humanity. Whether through acts of kindness, sharing knowledge, or fostering community, contributing to something bigger than yourself adds a profound layer to your greatness.

In essence, the concept of greatness within oneself is a call to self-discovery, self-acceptance, and personal growth. It's an acknowledgment that every individual has the capacity to lead a meaningful and impactful life by tapping into their inherent greatness. So, embark on the journey within, explore your uniqueness, embrace your strengths, face challenges with resilience, pursue your passions, and contribute positively to the world – for that is the path to discovering the greatness that lies within you.

Positive Transformations and Team Magic

Positive transformations and unity strength are like the sunshine breaking through the clouds, bringing warmth and brightness to the world around us. These concepts hold the power to uplift individuals and communities, fostering a sense of togetherness that can overcome challenges and create lasting change.

Positive Transformations

Positive transformations are the remarkable changes that occur when individuals or communities embrace optimism, growth, and constructive change. It's about turning challenges into opportunities, setbacks into lessons, and darkness into light. Imagine a caterpillar transforming into a beautiful butterfly – it undergoes a metamorphosis, emerging with newfound beauty and resilience. Similarly, positive transformations in human lives involve a process of self-discovery, learning, and evolving into the best version of oneself.

One aspect of positive transformations is the ability to adapt and learn from experiences. Life is a ride filled with twists and turns, and each experience, whether joyful or challenging, contributes to personal growth. Embracing a positive mindset allows individuals to see the silver lining in difficult situations, turning obstacles into stepping stones towards a brighter future.

Moreover, positive transformations often involve cultivating a mindset of gratitude. Gratitude is like a magic elixir that enhances our appreciation for the good things in life. It shifts focus from what is lacking to what is present, creating a ripple effect of positivity. By acknowledging and being thankful for the positive aspects of life, individuals can transform their perspectives and cultivate a more fulfilling existence.

Unity Strength

Unity strength is the formidable power that emerges when individuals join forces, working together towards common goals. It's the understanding that, collectively, we are stronger than we are individually. Picture a bundle of sticks – individually, they might be fragile, but when bound together, they become unbreakable. This strength in unity applies not only to individuals but also to communities, nations, and the global human family.

One fundamental aspect of unity strength is collaboration. When people come together, pooling their strengths and resources, they can achieve things that would be impossible alone. It's the synergy of diverse talents and perspectives creating a powerful force for positive change. Whether it's addressing social issues, promoting environmental sustainability, or advancing scientific discoveries, unity strength fuels progress.

Moreover, unity strength fosters a sense of belonging and support. In times of difficulty, individuals can draw strength from the collective resilience of their communities. This support network provides a safety net, encouraging individuals to face challenges with courage and perseverance. Together, people can weather storms, overcome obstacles, and celebrate victories, creating a sense of shared accomplishment.

The Interplay of Positive Transformations and Unity Strength

The beauty lies in the interplay between positive transformations and unity strength. Positive transformations within individuals contribute to the collective strength of a community, and conversely, the unity strength of a community can facilitate positive transformations on a larger scale.

Imagine a community that embraces positive transformations in its individuals – where personal growth, resilience, and gratitude become shared values. This community, fueled by the strength of unity, can then tackle challenges with a collective spirit, amplifying the impact of positive change.

In essence, positive transformations and unity strength complement each other in creating a harmonious and thriving society. It's a reminder that by fostering personal growth, cultivating a positive mindset, and embracing the strength of togetherness, we can build a better world for ourselves and future generations. Like a mosaic of individual pieces coming together to form a beautiful picture, positive transformations and unity of strength create a tapestry of hope, resilience, and shared success.

Chapter 2

Rings and Queens in History

In the stories of ancient times, there were powerful kings and queens who ruled with wisdom and bravery. Take Mansa Musa of Mali, a wealthy and generous king, or Queen Nefertiti, admired for her intelligence in ancient Egypt. King Shaka, a brilliant military mind in the Zulu Kingdom, and fearless Queen Amina of Zazzau in Nigeria are tales of strength. The wise Queen of Sheba's diplomacy and prosperity are legendary. These historical figures aren't just rulers; they're inspirations, teaching us about leadership, courage, and the rich tapestry of our shared history. Their legacies echo through time, timeless lessons for today.

Exploring the Rich History of African Kings and Queens

In the large and diverse continent of Africa, a rich tapestry of history unfolds, revealing the stories of extraordinary kings and queens who played key roles in determining the destinies of their people. These leaders weren't just rulers; they were visionaries, leaving behind legacies that continue to motivate and resonate.

Ancient Marvels: African Kingdoms and Their Royalty

Centuries ago, long before the buzz of modern cities and the whirl of technology, Africa was home to powerful kingdoms with leaders whose tales are woven into the fabric of time. These kingdoms were not only centers of trade and culture but also the domains of kings and queens who ruled with wisdom, courage, and a deep connection to their people.

Mansa Musa: The Wealthy Heart of Mali

Mansa Musa, the 14th-century Mali Empire's monarch, is one such notable person in African history. Known for his incredible wealth, Mansa Musa was not just a king; he was a symbol of benevolence. His kingdom, which spanned across West Africa, thrived under his leadership.

Mansa Musa is often hailed as one of the wealthiest individuals in history. His kingdom was a beacon of prosperity, and his fame reached far beyond the borders of Mali. What makes his story even more remarkable is not just his wealth but how he used it for the benefit of his people.

King Mansa Musa

Queen Nefertiti: Beauty and Leadership in Ancient Egypt

Moving to the northeastern part of Africa, we encounter the captivating Queen Nefertiti of ancient Egypt. Known not only for her beauty but also for her intelligence and leadership, Queen Nefertiti left an ineradicable mark on the cultural and political landscape of Egypt.

During her time, Egypt witnessed a flourishing of the arts and diplomacy. Nefertiti's influence extended beyond the royal court, and she played a noteworthy role in influencing the religious and cultural practices of the time. Her legacy, often depicted in ancient art and hieroglyphs, stands as a testament to the impact a queen could have in society.

Queen Nefertiti

Shaka: The Military Genius of the Zulu Kingdom

Heading south to the Zulu Kingdom, we encounter the legendary King Shaka, a military genius who reshaped the destiny of his people. Shaka's story is one of unification and strength, as he brought together various clans to form a formidable force.

What sets Shaka apart is not just his military prowess but also his innovative strategies. He introduced new tactics and weaponry, revolutionizing the way wars were fought in southern Africa. His legacy is not only evident in the military might of the Zulu Kingdom but also in the cultural heritage of the region.

King Shaka

Queen Amina: Warrior Queen of Zazzau

Venturing into the heart of Nigeria, we discover the fearless Queen Amina of Zazzau. Amina was not just a queen; she was a warrior who led her people with strength and courage. Her military campaigns expanded the kingdom's territory, and her strategic brilliance in battle is still remembered today.

Queen Amina's story challenges traditional gender roles. She wasn't confined to the palace; instead, she rode into battles, earning the respect of her subjects. Her legacy as a warrior queen remains a source of inspiration, especially for those who believe in breaking barriers.

Queen Amina

The Queen of Sheba: Wisdom and Prosperity

Our journey concludes in the legendary kingdom of Sheba, where the wise and prosperous Queen of Sheba ruled. Known for her keen sense of justice and diplomatic skills, she led her kingdom to unprecedented prosperity.

The Queen of Sheba's story goes beyond the riches of her kingdom. Her encounter with King Solomon, as recounted in various historical and religious texts, highlights her diplomatic acumen. The cultural exchange between the two rulers became a symbol of harmony and cooperation, transcending borders.

The Queen of Sheba

Why Their Stories Matter Today

The tales of these African kings and queens are not just chapters in history books; they are living legacies that continue to influence and inspire. In a world filled with challenges, their stories remind us of the resilience, wisdom, and leadership that can shape the course of nations.

Understanding the history of African kings and queens is crucial for appreciating the diverse and rich heritage of the continent. These stories challenge stereotypes and showcase the depth of African civilizations, contributing to a more nuanced and accurate understanding of Africa's past and present.

As we reflect on the accomplishments of these remarkable leaders, may their stories serve as beacons of inspiration. In a world that is often focused on the present and the future, delving into the history of African kings and queens allows us to connect with the roots of human civilization and appreciate the enduring impact of visionary leadership.

The Power of Positive Role Models

Imagine having someone to look up to, someone who

inspires you to be the best version of yourself. These special people are called positive role models, and they play a crucial role in our lives, guiding us with their good deeds, kind hearts, and inspiring actions. Let's delve into why having positive role models is like having guiding lights that brighten our paths.

Who Are Positive Role Models?

Positive role models are people we admire and learn from. They can be from all walks of life—parents, teachers, community leaders, or even famous figures. What makes them special is the positive influence they have on us. They show us how to be kind, work hard, and overcome challenges. Their actions speak louder than words, and we find ourselves wanting to follow in their footsteps.

Why Are Role Models Important?

Role models are like beacons of light in the darkness. They show us the way when things seem tough, and they give us hope when we face difficulties. Here's why having positive role models is so important:

1. **Inspiration to Dream Big:** Positive role models inspire us to dream big and aim for the stars. When we see someone we look up to achieving great things, it makes us believe that we can do it, too. They motivate us to set goals and work hard to reach them.

2. **Guidance in Making Good Choices:** Life is full of choices, and sometimes, it can be tricky to know what the right decision is. Positive role models help us navigate through these choices by showing us the importance of honesty, kindness, and responsibility. Their actions become a compass, guiding us toward making good decisions.

3. **Building Confidence:** Having someone we admire believing in us can boost our confidence. Positive role models encourage us to believe in ourselves and our abilities. Their support gives us the courage to face challenges and overcome obstacles.

4. **Learning Values and Morals:** Role models teach us about values and morals. They demonstrate kindness, empathy, and respect for others. By watching them, we learn how to be good and considerate people, making the world a better place.

5. **Resilience in Tough Times:** Life is not always smooth sailing; there are storms and challenges. Positive role models show us how to be resilient, how to bounce back from difficulties, and how to keep going even when things get tough. Their strength becomes a source of inspiration during our own struggles.

Real-Life Examples of Positive Role Models

Let's take a look at a few real-life examples of positive role models and understand how they impact our lives:

1. **Mom and Dad:** Our parents are often our first and most influential role models. They teach us about love, hard work, and responsibility. Watching them, we learn important life lessons that shape us into the individuals we become.

Becoming Positive Role Models

It's not just about looking up to others; it's also about becoming positive role models ourselves. As we grow, we have the power to influence those around us, especially younger siblings, friends, or classmates. Here's how we can be positive role models:

1. **Show Kindness:** Small acts of kindness, like helping a friend or being polite, make a big difference. By showing kindness, we inspire others to do the same.

2. **Work Hard:** Whether it's in school or in our hobbies, working hard and giving our best effort sets an example. Others see our determination and are encouraged to put in effort as well.

3. **Be Honest:** Honesty is a valuable trait. By being truthful and admitting mistakes, we show that integrity is important. Others will admire and learn from our honesty.

4. **Stay Positive:** Positivity is contagious. Even in difficult situations, maintaining a positive attitude helps us and those around us. It shows that we can find solutions and keep going, no matter what.

5. **Help Others:** Offering help to those in need, whether it's a classmate struggling with homework or a neighbor carrying groceries, demonstrates the importance of lending a helping hand.

As we look up to those who make a positive impact, let's also strive to be role models ourselves, spreading kindness, working hard, and making the world a better place for everyone.

Modern Inspirations

As we celebrate the legacies of historical figures, it's essential to recognize contemporary positive role models who continue to inspire us today. Let's briefly highlight the stories of a few modern individuals who have risen from humble beginnings, stayed focused, and achieved remarkable success:

Barack Obama

Barack Obama's journey from a community organizer to becoming the 44th President of the United States is a testament to the power of perseverance and the pursuit of a larger vision. Born in Honolulu, Hawaii, to a Kenyan father and a Kansan mother, Obama's early life was marked by multicultural influences. Despite facing challenges and setbacks, including racial prejudice, he excelled academically and rose through the political ranks with a message of hope, unity, and change.

Obama's presidency, from 2009 to 2017, was historic as he became the first African American to hold the highest office in the land. His leadership amid difficult circumstances, such as the financial crisis and the enactment of the Affordable Care Act, demonstrated resilience and a commitment to transformative change. Post-presidency, Barack Obama continues to advocate for social and political issues through his memoirs, public speeches, and the Obama Foundation.

Barack Obama

Michelle Obama

Born and raised in Chicago, Illinois, Michelle Obama became a contemporary symbol of activism, elegance, and brilliance. Her journey from a working-class family to becoming the First Lady of the United States is marked by a dedication to education, public service, and health and wellness.

Michelle Obama's initiatives as First Lady, including the "Let's Move!" drive to fight childhood obesity and the "Reach Higher" program encouraging higher education, showcased her commitment to the well-being of the nation's youth. Much like myself, Michelle Obama emphasized the importance of addressing childhood obesity. My efforts to combat this issue are reflected in my books, *"The ABCs Of Healthy Foods, Plants, And Wild Animals: Part I and II,"* which aim to promote healthy lifestyles and educate children about nutrition and wellness. Her impact extended beyond traditional roles, emphasizing the importance of community engagement and the power of individual agency.

Since leaving the White House, Michelle Obama has continued her advocacy work. Her memoir, "Becoming," became a bestseller, providing a candid and inspiring account of her life. Through the Obama Foundation, she focuses on initiatives promoting education, leadership, and civic engagement.

Michelle Obama

Oprah Winfrey

Oprah Winfrey's life story is a remarkable journey from poverty to becoming a media magnate. Born in rural Mississippi, she faced adversity and hardship in her early years. However, her determination, resilience, and passion for storytelling propelled her to success. Oprah is best recognized for hosting "The Oprah Winfrey Show," which became a cultural phenomenon. She later founded her own media company, Harpo Productions, and has expanded her influence into various philanthropic endeavors. Oprah's story is often cited as an inspiration for overcoming obstacles and achieving greatness through hard work and dedication.

Oprah Winfrey

Tyler Perry

Tyler Perry's life is a testament to the transformative power of personal determination and creativity. Raised in a challenging environment, Perry used his difficult experiences as fuel for his artistic endeavors. He gained prominence with his stage plays and later transitioned to filmmaking, creating the popular Madea film series. Perry's success is not only measured in his achievements as a filmmaker, playwright, and actor but also in his impact on promoting diversity and representation in the entertainment industry. His story exemplifies the possibilities that arise when one channelizes adversity into creative expression and determination.

Tyler Perry

Jeff Bezos

Jeff Bezos, the founder of Amazon, commenced his entrepreneurial journey by establishing an online bookstore in 1994. Over the years, Bezos transformed Amazon into an e-commerce giant and diversified its offerings into various sectors, including cloud computing, streaming services, and artificial intelligence. Bezos' innovative thinking, risk-taking, and customer-centric approach have played a pivotal role in Amazon's success. His story illustrates the power of visionary leadership, adaptability, and the ability to disrupt traditional business models.

Jeff Bezos

Mark Zuckerberg

Mark Zuckerberg co-founded Facebook in 2004, forever altering the landscape of social networking. His vision and programming skills led to the creation of a platform that connects people globally. Facebook's rapid growth made Zuckerberg one of the youngest billionaires in the world. His journey is a reflection of the impact technology can have on society, as well as the potential of innovative ideas to shape the way people communicate and share information. However, Zuckerberg's success is not without controversy, as Facebook has faced scrutiny for its influence on privacy, misinformation, and societal issues.

Mark Zuckerberg

Why Do Their Stories Matter Today?

The stories of Oprah Winfrey, Tyler Perry, Jeff Bezos, and Mark Zuckerberg remain highly relevant and impactful today. They serve as beacons of inspiration, illustrating the triumph of resilience, determination, and hard work over adversity. Tyler Perry's success in the entertainment industry is particularly noteworthy, emphasizing the importance of diversity and representation. Jeff Bezos and Mark Zuckerberg embody the entrepreneurial spirit and showcase the transformative power of innovation in the realms of e-commerce and social networking. Oprah Winfrey's transition from media mogul to philanthropist underscores the social responsibility that accompanies success. Furthermore, Mark Zuckerberg's creation of Facebook continues to shape discussions on technology's role in society, addressing issues such as privacy and misinformation. These narratives collectively contribute to ongoing dialogues about success, diversity, innovation, and social impact, making their stories relevant and influential in our contemporary context.

Chapter 3

Who Am I?

From childhood blank canvas to the exploratory teenage years, our journey involves trying on different hats, like experimenting with hobbies and friendships adding pieces to our identity puzzle. Self-awareness acts like a flashlight, helping us understand our feelings and thoughts. It's like looking into a mirror, not just to see our reflection but to truly understand who we are. As life unfolds, our identity evolves, shaped by challenges and experiences, just like a river's ever-changing course.

Identity and Self-Awareness

Identity and self-awareness are like the pieces of a puzzle that make us unique individuals. In the journey of life, we often find ourselves pondering the question, "Who am I?" This exploration of identity is like embarking on a fascinating adventure, discovering the various facets that shape our sense of self.

At its core, identity is the sum of our characteristics, experiences, and beliefs that distinguish us from others. It's like a fingerprint, distinct and exclusive to each person. As we navigate the twists and turns of life, our identity evolves, influenced by the people we meet, the places we go, and the challenges we overcome.

Self-awareness, on the other hand, is the flashlight that helps us illuminate the depths of our own being. It's the ability to introspect and understand our emotions, thoughts, and actions. Picture it as looking into a mirror not just to see your reflection but to truly comprehend the essence within. This self-awareness is a key element in the puzzle of identity.

As children, our identity is like a blank painting waiting to be painted with the colors of experiences. We start forming connections with our family, learning about our cultural background, and discovering our likes and dislikes. However, it's not until adolescence that the exploration of identity takes center stage. We begin to question our beliefs, challenge societal norms, and forge our own paths.

The journey of self-discovery is not always smooth. It involves moments of confusion, self-doubt, and even reinvention. Think of it as trying on different hats until we find the one that fits perfectly. This process may involve experimenting with various hobbies, exploring different friendships, or even delving into diverse cultures. Each experience adds a piece to the puzzle, contributing to the complexity and richness of our identity.

Identity is not a static concept; it's dynamic and fluid. Just as a river constantly flows and evolves, so does our sense of self. Life experiences act as the currents shaping the riverbed, carving out the contours of our identity. Sometimes, we may find unexpected sources of strength within ourselves during challenging times, realizing capabilities we never knew existed.

In the age of technology and social media, the exploration of identity takes on new dimensions. We craft online personas, curate digital versions of ourselves, and connect with a global community. However, amidst the digital noise, it becomes crucial to sift through the virtual identities and rediscover the authentic self. True self-awareness is not about the number of followers or likes but about understanding our values, passions, and aspirations.

Moreover, the theme of identity extends beyond the individual to encompass societal and cultural dimensions. It's like a mosaic, with each person contributing a distinctive piece that, when combined, forms a beautiful picture. Embracing diversity and recognizing the value of different identities enriches the collective human experience.

Unlocking Your Greatness

Let's take a moment to think about your potential. Yes, yours! It's easy to underestimate ourselves or think that greatness is only for a chosen few. But what if we shift our focus and consider the untapped greatness within each of us?

Take a moment to question those thoughts that tell you what you can or cannot do. What if you believed in yourself a bit more? What if you had the confidence to pursue your dreams? It's time to challenge those preconceived notions about your capabilities and limitations.

There are countless ordinary people who have achieved extraordinary feats. They are not superheroes; they are individuals just like you and me. Their stories remind us that greatness is not exclusive—it's a potential within everyone. Yes, including you!

Now, let's talk about personal growth and self-discovery. These are not one-time events; they are ongoing processes. Imagine a journey where you embrace challenges and learn from failures, where setbacks become opportunities for growth.

Every stumble is a chance to rise stronger. Imagine a seed pushing through the soil to become a mighty tree. Similarly, each challenge you face is a step toward unlocking your potential. It's about resilience and determination, qualities that grow stronger with every experience.

Think about a time when you faced a setback. Did it feel like the end, or did it open a door to new possibilities? Reflect on the lessons you learned and the strengths you gained. That's the beauty of setbacks—they can be stepping stones to your greater self.

From Rejection to Wizardry: J.K. Rowling's Inspirational Journey of Perseverance and Literary Triumph

Consider the story of J.K. Rowling, the author of the Harry Potter series. Before her books became a global phenomenon, Rowling faced numerous rejections from publishers. She was a struggling single mother, battling financial difficulties and self-doubt. Many would have seen her situation as a limitation, but Rowling saw it as an opportunity to pursue her passion for writing. Her perseverance and belief in her storytelling abilities eventually led to one of the most successful literary franchises in history.

J.K. Rowling's journey from a struggling single mother to the globally celebrated author of the Harry Potter series is an inspiring tale of resilience, willpower, and the influence of believing in oneself.

Before the magic of Hogwarts captivated readers worldwide, Rowling experienced a series of setbacks. She faced rejection from multiple publishers, each one turning down the manuscript of her first book. It would have been easy for her to see these rejections as insurmountable obstacles, but Rowling viewed them as stepping stones on her path to success.

J.K. Rowling

It's essential to note that Rowling's passion for writing and storytelling fueled her resilience. She didn't let the circumstances define her or limit her aspirations. Instead, she used her difficult situation as an opportunity to channel her creativity and bring her imagination to life. Writing became a therapeutic outlet and a source of solace amid the struggles.

The turning point came when Bloomsbury, a small publishing house, decided to take a chance on Rowling's debut novel, "Harry Potter and the Philosopher's Stone." The book, later released as "Harry Potter and the Sorcerer's Stone" in the United States, marked the beginning of an extraordinary journey. The success of the first book paved the way for the entire series, turning Rowling into a literary sensation and a household name.

Rowling's story teaches us valuable lessons about perseverance, self-belief, and the importance of embracing challenges as opportunities for growth. Her journey underscores the idea that setbacks and failures are not the end of the road but rather stepping stones toward success.

Furthermore, Rowling's success goes beyond the realm of literature; it has had a profound impact on popular culture. The Harry Potter series has turned out to be a cultural phenomenon, spawning movies, merchandise, theme parks, and a dedicated fan base. Rowling's ability to weave a compelling narrative resonated with people of all ages, transcending borders and cultural differences.

In essence, J.K. Rowling's story serves as a testament to the idea that passion, coupled with unwavering determination, can overcome seemingly insurmountable challenges. It encourages aspiring individuals to pursue their dreams persistently, regardless of the difficulties they may encounter along the way. Rowling's journey is a reminder that success often comes to those who refuse to be defined by their circumstances and instead choose to define their own destiny through hard work, perseverance, and an unshakeable belief in their abilities.

The Innate Power Within Every Individual

In a world where external achievements often take center stage, it is essential to recognize and embrace the profound idea that greatness resides within each individual. This intrinsic potential, often overlooked in the pursuit of societal benchmarks, is a force waiting to be unleashed, transforming ordinary lives into extraordinary journeys.

DISCOVERING GREATNESS

At the core of this concept lies the belief that every person possesses a unique set of talents, capabilities, and untapped potential that can contribute to personal fulfillment and societal progress. It challenges the conventional narrative that greatness is reserved for a select few, emphasizing that it is a universal birthright waiting to be discovered and nurtured.

Human history is replete with stories of individuals who defied societal expectations and discovered their greatness within. From the artistic brilliance of Leonardo da Vinci to the scientific genius of Marie Curie, these luminaries exemplify the power of unlocking one's inherent greatness. However, the journey to self-discovery and unleashing one's potential is not limited to the extraordinary. It is a narrative that transcends boundaries, applicable to individuals from all walks of life.

Understanding that greatness is within each individual requires a shift in perspective, challenging the ingrained notion that success is measured solely by external achievements. It involves recognizing that personal growth, resilience, and the pursuit of passion are integral components of greatness. The journey begins by acknowledging one's strengths, weaknesses, and unique qualities, laying the foundation for self-awareness and acceptance.

In the pursuit of greatness, individuals often encounter obstacles that test their resolve. These challenges serve as opportunities for growth and self-discovery. Overcoming adversity is not only a testament to one's inner strength but also a pathway to unleashing latent greatness. It is in these moments of struggle that individuals tap into reservoirs of resilience and courage, uncovering aspects of their character that were previously dormant.

Furthermore, the idea of greatness within each individual highlights the significance of raising a growth mindset. Embracing a mindset that views challenges as opportunities for learning and development opens doors to continuous improvement. It inspires people to step outside their comfort zones, explore new horizons, and cultivate the skills necessary for personal and professional growth.

Moreover, recognizing greatness within oneself fosters a sense of empowerment and accountability. It instills the belief that individuals have the agency to shape their destinies and make meaningful contributions to the world. This empowerment is not contingent on external validation but rather emerges from an authentic understanding of one's worth and potential.

The concept that greatness is within each individual is a powerful paradigm shift that has the potential to redefine how we perceive success and fulfillment. The realization that greatness is not reserved for the few but is a universal birthright opens the door to a world where every individual can contribute their unique gifts, making a collective impact on the tapestry of human experience.

Chapter 4
The Power of Unity

Ever heard about the incredible strength that comes from sticking together? That's what unity is all about. It's like everyone joining hands and working as one big team. This idea is super important in our daily lives, whether we're talking about families, communities, or even when people work together on cool technology stuff. The real magic of unity, though, is how it helps us overcome challenges and achieve big goals. It's like when friends help each other out or when a whole bunch of people work together to make things better.

The Power of Unity Across Personal, Community, and Technological Dimensions

Unity is a concept that holds immense significance in various aspects of life, fostering cooperation, collaboration, and togetherness among individuals or groups. At its core, unity refers to the state of being united or joined together, emphasizing a sense of oneness and shared purpose. This fundamental idea transcends boundaries, whether in personal relationships, communities, or even in the world of technology.

In personal relationships, unity plays a crucial role in creating a strong and supportive foundation. It involves individuals coming together, sharing common values, and working towards shared goals. In families, for instance, unity creates a harmonious environment where members support and uplift each other through thick and thin. This shared strength not only fortifies relationships but also helps individuals face challenges with resilience and determination.

Community unity is another facet of this concept, bringing people together for the greater good. Communities thrive when individuals set aside differences and collaborate toward common objectives. This sense of togetherness promotes social cohesion, leading to a safer and more vibrant living environment. Whether it's a neighborhood coming together to address common concerns or a society working collectively to achieve progress, unity is the catalyst that propels positive change.

Beyond personal and community aspects, unity holds great importance in the world of technology, particularly in the realm of game development through platforms like Unity. Unity, in this context, is a powerful game development engine that allows creators to build interactive and immersive experiences. It brings together various elements like graphics, physics, and scripting, unifying them into a seamless whole. The strength of Unity lies in its ability to integrate diverse components, fostering collaboration among different elements to create a cohesive and functional game.

The power that arises from unity is evident in its capability to overcome trials and achieve goals that might seem insurmountable when faced alone. It magnifies individual strengths, creating a collective force that is greater than the sum of its parts. This strength can be observed in various aspects of life, from personal achievements to societal progress and technological advancements.

Unity is a concept that binds individuals, communities, and even elements of technology together. Its significance is profound, promoting collaboration, fostering strength, and enabling the accomplishment of shared goals. Whether in personal relationships, communities, or the realm of technology, unity is a force that propels progress and creates a foundation for resilience and success.

The Unyielding Power of Unity in Shaping Societal Milestones

Throughout history, unity has proven to be a powerful force that has shaped the course of societies and led to significant milestones. Many instances demonstrate how movements, revolutions, and social changes were driven by a collective sense of unity, highlighting the immense impact that coming together can have on achieving common goals.

One prominent historical example of unity shaping the course of events is the American Revolution in the late 18th century. Colonists in the thirteen American colonies faced numerous challenges and grievances against British rule. However, it was the unity among the colonists that allowed them to stand together against a common oppressor. The collecting cry of "no taxation without representation" echoed through the colonies, uniting people from diverse backgrounds and beliefs in their quest for independence. This shared sense of purpose and unity ultimately led to the formation of the United States of America.

Similarly, the Civil Rights Movement in the mid-20th century in the United States is another compelling illustration of how unity can drive social change. African Americans, along with allies from different racial backgrounds, came together to fight against racial segregation and discrimination. Figures like Martin Luther King Jr. inspired millions with their calls for unity and equality. The Civil Rights Movement's success in challenging systemic racism was a testament to the power of unity in bringing about transformative societal shifts.

Moving to more recent history, the fall of the Berlin Wall in 1989 serves as a powerful example of how unity can break down physical and ideological barriers. The wall, which had divided East and West Berlin for nearly three decades, symbolized the Cold War's division between communist and capitalist ideologies. The unified efforts of the people, demanding freedom and the reunification of their city, played a crucial role in bringing down the oppressive barrier. The fall of the Berlin Wall was the end of the Cold War era and signified the triumph of unity over division.

In all these historical examples, unity emerged as a driving force behind significant milestones. Whether in the fight for independence, civil rights, or the dismantling of oppressive structures, the power of people coming together cannot be overstated. These instances underscore the enduring truth that unity has the potential to overcome even the most formidable challenges, inspiring collective action and paving the way for transformative change in societies throughout history.

Unity in Action

Unity, a concept as old as humanity itself, carries immense significance in our daily lives. It transcends borders, cultures, and backgrounds, bringing people together in pursuit of common goals. We will delve into the concept of unity through relatable real-life examples that showcase its transformative power.

Community Strength

One striking example of unity is evident in communities that come together during challenging times. Natural calamities, such as storms, earthquakes, or floods, often serve as catalysts for people to unite. In such situations, individuals from diverse backgrounds set aside differences to provide support and assistance. Neighbors help each other rebuild homes, share resources, and offer emotional support, illustrating how unity can turn adversity into an opportunity for collective resilience.

Global Collaborations

The world has witnessed the power of unity on a global scale through collaborative efforts to address pressing issues. Before delving into the challenges posed by the COVID-19 pandemic, it's crucial to acknowledge another significant movement that underscored the need for global solidarity—the Black Lives Matter movement of 2020. The world came together across races to condemn an unjust court system and instances of police brutality. This call for unity emphasized that the struggle for equality persists and affects us all as a human race. In a symbolic act, a mural in Bed-Stuy, New York City, marked the streets with giant yellow letters spelling out "Black Lives Matter," not to diminish the value of other lives but to spotlight the ongoing daily struggles faced by one particular race. Returning to the global perspective, the response to the COVID-19 pandemic further exemplifies the necessity of unified efforts. Countries, despite geopolitical differences, collaborated to develop and distribute vaccines, exchange crucial information, and offer medical assistance. The pandemic illustrated that global challenges demand collective unity for effective solutions, reinforcing the interconnectedness of humanity.

Civil Rights Movements

History provides us with powerful examples of unity fueling social change. The Civil Rights Movement in the United States during the 1950s and 1960s is a prime illustration. Individuals from diverse racial and ethnic backgrounds united to demand equal rights and an end to racial segregation. Through peaceful protests, marches, and acts of civil disobedience, the movement paved the way for legislative changes that continue to shape societal norms today. This historical example underscores how unity can dismantle deeply ingrained systemic injustices.

Corporate Success

Unity is not limited to social or political spheres; it is equally pivotal in the business world. Successful companies often attribute their achievements to a cohesive and unified workforce. When employees share a common vision, collaborate effectively, and support each other, they create a positive work environment that fosters innovation and productivity. The success of companies like Google, known for its collaborative workplace culture, exemplifies how unity can be a driving force behind organizational accomplishments.

Family Bonds

At its core, unity begins within the family unit. Families serve as microcosms of society, and their dynamics greatly influence an individual's understanding of unity. In times of joy or sorrow, families that stand united demonstrate resilience and love. Supporting each other through challenges, celebrating achievements together, and fostering open communication are essential aspects of family unity. These principles, when extended beyond the family unit, contribute to the broader fabric of societal cohesion.

Sportsmanship

The world of sports provides a unique platform to witness the concept of unity in action. Teams, comprising individuals with different skills and backgrounds, work together to achieve a common objective. The success of a team often hinges on the ability of its members to unite, communicate effectively, and support one another. The Olympic Games, a global sporting event, exemplify unity on an international scale as athletes from diverse nations compete with respect for one another, transcending geopolitical differences.

Environmental Conservation

Unity is also integral to addressing global challenges like environmental conservation. The threats posed by climate change necessitate collective efforts from individuals, communities, and nations. Initiatives such as reforestation projects, waste reduction campaigns, and sustainable practices require unified action to make a meaningful impact. By recognizing the shared responsibility for the planet, people worldwide can contribute to preserving the environment for future generations.

The concept of unity permeates various aspects of our lives, offering a powerful framework for positive change. From local communities to global collaborations, from civil rights movements to family bonds, unity serves as a catalyst for progress and resilience. Real-life examples underscore the transformative potential of unity, encouraging us to embrace collective efforts for a better, more interconnected world. As we navigate the complexities of our existence, let us draw inspiration from these examples and recognize that unity remains a timeless and universal force that shapes our shared human experience.

Chapter 5

African American History for Kids

African American history is a narrative of resilience, struggle, triumph, and cultural brilliance. It is a tale that spans centuries, encompassing a diverse range of experiences that have shaped not only the African American community but the entire trajectory of American history.

The Era of Slavery

Our journey begins in the dark period of slavery, a time when millions of Africans were forcibly brought to the Americas under brutal conditions. The transatlantic slave trade cast a long shadow over the nation's history, leaving scars that continue to be felt today. The resilience of enslaved individuals, however, laid the foundation for the African American spirit.

Key Figures:

1. Harriet Tubman: Often referred to as the "Moses of her people," Tubman was a conductor of the Underground Railroad, leading hundreds of enslaved individuals to freedom.

2. Frederick Douglass: A former slave turned abolitionist, Douglass became a powerful orator and writer, advocating for the abolition of slavery.

The Civil War and Emancipation

The Civil War marked a turning point in American history, with the Emancipation Proclamation in 1863 declaring enslaved individuals in Confederate states free. The struggle for equality, however, was far from over.

Key Figures:

1. Abraham Lincoln: The 16th President of the United States, Lincoln played a pivotal role in the abolition of slavery through the Emancipation Proclamation.

2. Sojourner Truth: A prominent abolitionist and women's rights advocate, Truth delivered the powerful "Ain't I a Woman?" speech, challenging gender and racial inequalities.

Reconstruction and Jim Crow Era

The aftermath of the Civil War witnessed the Reconstruction era, where efforts were made to integrate formerly enslaved individuals into society. However, the rise of Jim Crow laws instituted segregation, perpetuating racial discrimination.

Key Figures:

1. Booker T. Washington: A prominent educator and civil rights leader, Washington founded the Tuskegee Institute and advocated for vocational training and economic self-sufficiency.

2. W.E.B. Du Bois: A co-founder of the National Association for the Advancement of Colored People (NAACP), Du Bois emphasized higher education and political activism to achieve civil rights

The Harlem Renaissance

The 20th century brought about a cultural and artistic explosion known as the Harlem Renaissance. African American intellectuals, artists, and musicians thrived in an atmosphere that celebrated black identity and creativity.

Key Figures:

1. Langston Hughes: A leading figure of the Harlem Renaissance, Hughes was a poet, novelist, and playwright known for his contributions to African American literature.

2. Duke Ellington: Renowned as a jazz composer and bandleader, Ellington's music transcended racial boundaries, contributing to the cultural fabric of the nation.

The Civil Rights Movement

The mid-20th century saw a seismic shift in the fight for civil rights as African Americans sought to dismantle institutionalized racism and segregation.

Key Figures:

1. Martin Luther King Jr.: A Baptist minister and civil

rights leader, King played a central role in the American civil rights movement, advocating for nonviolent protest and equality.

2. Rosa Parks: Frequently known as the "Mother of the Civil Rights Movement," Parks sparked the Montgomery Bus Boycott by refusing to give up her bus seat to a white passenger.

Martin Luther King Jr.

Contemporary Struggles and Achievements

The journey through African American history extends to contemporary times, with ongoing struggles against systemic racism and continued achievements in various fields.

Key Figures:

1. Barack Obama: In 2008, Barack Obama made history as the first African American President of the United States, symbolizing progress while acknowledging the work that still needed to be done.

2. Kamala Harris: In 2021, Kamala Harris became the first woman, first African American woman, and first Asian American woman to serve as Vice President of the United States, breaking multiple barriers.

Kamala Harris

Learning from the Past

As we reflect on this journey through African American history, it becomes evident that the past is a powerful teacher. Learning from the struggles and triumphs of those who came before us is essential for fostering a more just and equitable society. The concept of learning from the past involves acknowledging the mistakes of history, understanding the root causes of societal issues, and actively working towards positive change.

1. Acknowledging Historical Injustices: Understanding the history of African Americans requires a candid acknowledgment of the historical injustices they endured, including slavery, segregation, and systemic discrimination. By confronting this difficult past, society can move toward reconciliation and healing.

2. Embracing Diversity and Inclusion: African American history is not a separate narrative but an integral part of the broader American story. Embracing diversity and fostering inclusion is not only a moral imperative but also a means of

strengthening the social fabric and ensuring a more equitable future for all.

3. **Empowering Through Education:** Education is a powerful tool for dismantling ignorance and prejudice. Integrating a comprehensive and accurate representation of African American history into educational curricula ensures that future generations are equipped with a nuanced understanding of the nation's past.

4. **Advocating for Social Justice:** The struggles of the past serve as a call to action for present and future generations. Advocating for social justice involves actively challenging systemic inequalities, speaking out against discrimination, and working towards policies that promote equality for all.

By examining the key figures and events that shaped this history, we gain insights into the struggles and triumphs that have contributed to the fabric of American society. As we learn from the past, we are compelled to actively participate in the ongoing journey toward a more just, inclusive, and equitable future. African American history is not just a chapter in the nation's story; it is a crucial thread that weaves through the entire tapestry, reminding us of the collective responsibility to learn, grow, and strive for a better tomorrow.

Chapter 6
The Cultural Lights Movement

In human experience, cultural diversity stands as a vibrant and integral thread, weaving together the stories, traditions, and perspectives that make our world rich and multifaceted. The idea of cultural enlightenment and appreciation serves as a gateway to understanding, fostering a deep respect for the myriad ways people express their identities.

Cultural Enlightenment

Cultural enlightenment is a concept that goes beyond mere awareness; it involves an active and empathetic engagement with the various facets of different cultures. It is a journey that encourages individuals to move beyond their own cultural boundaries, exploring the traditions, art, language, and customs that shape the lives of others.

1. **Cultural Appreciation vs. Appropriation:** Cultural enlightenment begins with distinguishing between appreciation and appropriation. Appreciation involves genuinely valuing and

respecting cultural elements, acknowledging their significance without diminishing their meaning. On the other hand, appropriation involves borrowing cultural elements without understanding or respecting their context, often leading to misrepresentation and harm.

2. **The Power of Cross-Cultural Communication:** Embracing cultural enlightenment is synonymous with fostering effective cross-cultural communication. This involves recognizing and understanding cultural nuances, communication styles, and non-verbal cues. Through open dialogue and a willingness to learn, individuals can bridge gaps, dispel stereotypes, and build connections across diverse communities.

The Importance of Celebrating Diversity

Celebrating diversity is not just a slogan; it is a fundamental pillar of a harmonious and inclusive society. Diversity encompasses differences in ethnicity, race, religion, gender, sexual orientation, and more. Acknowledging and appreciating these differences contributes to the richness of human experience and promotes a more tolerant and open-minded world.

1. **Cultural Diversity as a Strength:** Diversity is a strength that propels societies forward. A variety of perspectives and experiences foster innovation, creativity, and resilience. Organizations, communities, and nations that embrace diversity in all its forms are better equipped to address complex challenges and adapt to an ever-evolving global landscape.

2. **Cultural Festivals and Celebrations:** Cultural festivals and celebrations provide vibrant avenues for showcasing diversity. These events serve as platforms for communities to share their traditions, art, music, and cuisine. Attending or participating in these celebrations allows individuals to gain firsthand experiences and forge connections with people from different cultural backgrounds.

Embracing and Understanding Different Cultures

Embracing and understanding different cultures

requires a proactive and open-minded approach. It involves stepping out of one's comfort zone, challenging preconceived notions, and engaging with diverse perspectives. By doing so, individuals not only enrich their own lives but contribute to building a more inclusive and interconnected global community.

1. **Cultural Empathy:** Cultivating cultural empathy involves putting oneself in the shoes of others seeking to understand their experiences, challenges, and aspirations. This emotional connection builds bridges of understanding and helps break down stereotypes and biases.

2. **Educational Initiatives:** Formal and informal education plays a crucial role in promoting cultural understanding. Introducing diverse curricula, literature, and history in schools fosters an early appreciation for different cultures. Educational initiatives that expose individuals to a global perspective contribute to creating informed and culturally literate citizens.

3. **Travel as a Catalyst for Cultural Understanding:** Travel provides a unique opportunity for cultural immersion. A person's viewpoint is expanded, and a greater understanding of the unique human experience is fostered via personal exposure to various cultures, interactions with locals, and observation of daily life in various places.

Overcoming Challenges to Cultural Enlightenment

While the benefits of cultural enlightenment are immense, it is vital to admit and address the challenges that may arise. Overcoming stereotypes, prejudices, and systemic barriers requires collective effort and a commitment to fostering an inclusive and tolerant society.

1. **Combatting Stereotypes and Prejudices:** Stereotypes and prejudices often stem from ignorance and lack of exposure. Education and awareness drives can play a pivotal role in challenging and dismantling these harmful narratives, encouraging individuals to question assumptions and embrace diversity.

2. **Promoting Inclusive Policies:** Organizations and institutions can contribute to cultural enlightenment by implementing inclusive policies that promote diversity at all levels. This includes hiring practices that consider diverse backgrounds, creating inclusive environments, and providing resources for cultural education.

In conclusion, cultural enlightenment and appreciation are not mere abstract ideals but guiding principles that can transform societies and individuals alike. By celebrating diversity and actively seeking to understand different cultures, we contribute to a global narrative that values inclusion, mutual respect, and shared humanity. In an interconnected world, the ability to navigate and appreciate diverse cultures is not just a skill; it is an essential aspect of fostering a more compassionate and harmonious coexistence. As we embark on the journey of cultural enlightenment, let us embrace the beauty of our differences and unite in our shared commitment to building a world that cherishes, respects, and learns from the kaleidoscope of human cultures.

Chapter 7

Empowering Through Thought

Just like superheroes have the power to change the world with their thoughts, you, too, can make a big difference by believing in yourself and having a positive attitude.

Imagine your mind as a treasure chest full of amazing ideas and possibilities. When you think good thoughts, it's like unlocking the treasure and discovering all the incredible things you can do. If you believe in your abilities and dream big, you'll find that you can overcome challenges and achieve anything you set your mind to!

Empowering through thought is not just about you; it's also about being a superhero for your friends and family. By sharing positive vibes and encouraging words, you can create a team of empowered thinkers who support each other on this exciting journey of life.

The Power of Positive Thinking

Positive thinking is like a special tool that helps us navigate through life's adventures with a brighter perspective. It's not just wishful thinking; it's a powerful mindset that can influence how we feel, act, and even achieve our goals.

Imagine your mind as a garden, and your thoughts are the seeds you plant. Positive thoughts are like seeds that grow into beautiful flowers, making your garden colorful and pleasant. When you focus on positive thoughts, you're nurturing your mental garden, creating a more enjoyable environment for yourself and those around you.

Positive thinking doesn't mean ignoring problems. Instead, it's about approaching challenges with a can-do attitude. When faced with difficulties, positive thinking encourages us to believe in our abilities and find solutions. It's like having a toolbox filled with problem-solving skills that help us overcome obstacles.

Affirmations, another aspect of positive thinking, are like special messages we tell ourselves. Saying things like "I am capable" or "I can learn from mistakes" is like programming our minds with positive beliefs. These affirmations act as a guiding light, reminding us of our strengths and encouraging us to face challenges confidently.

The language of positive thinking also extends to the way we communicate with others. Offering kind words and smiles is like sharing the magic of positivity. It generates a ripple effect, spreading joy and creating a more uplifting atmosphere in our homes, schools, and communities.

One fascinating aspect of positive thinking is its connection to resilience. Resilience is the skill to bounce back from hindrances, and positive thinking plays a crucial role in developing this skill. When we view mistakes as opportunities to learn and grow, we become more resilient, turning challenges into stepping stones for success.

Consider the idea that our thoughts can influence the outcomes we attract. This is often referred to as the "law of attraction." In simpler terms, when we focus on positive expectations, we tend to notice more positive opportunities and experiences. It's like having a magnet that attracts good things into our lives.

Positive thinking also acts as a shield against negativity. Just as we wear protective gear when riding a bike, positive thinking serves as a mental shield. When faced with negative comments or self-doubt, our positive mindset helps us deflect those thoughts and maintain a healthy sense of confidence.

Turning "I can't" into "I'll give it a try" exemplifies the growth mindset associated with positive thinking. Embracing challenges with a positive attitude opens doors to new possibilities. It encourages a love for learning and a belief that with effort and perseverance, we can achieve great things.

Positive thinking is a valuable tool that shapes our mindset and influences our experiences. By nurturing our mental garden with positive thoughts, using affirmations, and approaching challenges with optimism, we not only enhance our well-being but also create a more positive and resilient path for our educational journey and beyond.

Inspiring Stories of Overcoming Challenges Through Positive Mindset

In the big picture of life, people stand out not just because of what they've achieved but because they've faced tough times and bounced back with a positive mindset. These stories of staying strong and determined are like guiding lights, reminding us that even when things get tough, there's hope.

Michael Jordan: Defying Setbacks Through a Positive Mindset

In the realm of sports, the story of Michael Jordan is a testament to the triumph of the human spirit. Commonly considered one of the greatest basketball players of all time, Jordan faced numerous setbacks early in his career. Deemed too short by his high school coach, he used these setbacks as fuel to prove doubters wrong.

Jordan's secret weapon was his positive mindset. His famous words, "I can accept failure, everyone fails at something. But I can't accept not trying," propelled him to six NBA championships and five MVP awards. Jordan's resilience and unwavering belief in his abilities stand as an enduring example of the transformative power of a positive mindset.

Michael Jordan

Nelson Mandela: A Political Icon's Positive Outlook

In the political arena, Nelson Mandela's story is a shining example of triumph over adversity. Mandela, a pivotal player in the South African resistance to apartheid, was imprisoned for 27 years due to his political convictions. Instead of succumbing to bitterness, he emerged with a remarkable spirit of forgiveness and reconciliation.

Mandela's positive mindset played a pivotal role in South Africa's peaceful transition to democracy. Believing in the power of forgiveness and unity, he steered his country away from civil unrest. Mandela's ability to maintain a positive outlook amid immense personal sacrifice serves as a guiding light for those navigating challenges on the path to a better world.

Nelson Mandela

Nick Vujicic

Nick Vujicic, born without arms and legs, could have easily succumbed to a life defined by limitations. However, his story is a demonstration of the incredible strength of the human spirit. Instead of dwelling on what he lacked, Vujicic embraced a positive mindset that propelled him to become a motivational speaker, author, and evangelist.

Vujicic's journey of self-acceptance and positivity began with overcoming personal insecurities and societal prejudices. He realized that his worth was not determined by physical attributes but by the strength of his character and the power of his mindset. Through his speaking engagements and books, Vujicic shares his message of hope, encouraging others to embrace their uniqueness and overcome challenges with a positive perspective.

One of Vujicic's famous quotes encapsulates his philosophy: "I don't need easy. I just need possible." His narrative offers motivation to those confronting obstacles that appear insurmountable, reminding us that with a positive mindset, even the seemingly impossible can become achievable.

These stories teach us that having a positive mindset can make a big difference in our own lives. No matter what problems we face – whether it's money troubles, personal issues, or work challenges – thinking positively can guide us to solutions and open new doors. Just like Michael Jordan, Nelson Mandela, and Nick Vujicic, we all have the power to achieve amazing things when we stay positive and believe in a better future.

Embrace the exciting journey of learning with a growth mindset. See challenges not as roadblocks but as opportunities to develop and improve. Remember, it's okay to make mistakes—they're valuable lessons on the path to success. Celebrate your efforts and hard work, for they are the keys to unlocking your full potential. Cultivate a love for learning, curiosity, and the belief that your intelligence can grow through dedication and resilience. Your abilities are not fixed; they can expand with each new experience. So, face challenges with enthusiasm, view setbacks as stepping stones, and let the thrill of continuous learning guide you toward a future filled with possibilities.

Nick Vujicic

Chapter 8

Taking Away Truths

As we embark on the final chapter of our journey, let us distill the essence of the profound messages woven through the tapestry of this exploration. The chapters preceding have taken us on a voyage of self-discovery, cultural appreciation, unity, and positive thinking. Now, in "Taking Away Truths," we crystallize the key messages that resonate universally, echoing the fundamental belief that greatness is not a distant summit but an inherent birthright within every individual.

Being Great Is for Everyone: First things first, being great isn't just for a few lucky folks. It's for you, me, and everyone else. We've got something unique in us that adds to the coolness of the world. So, recognize it, own it, and let's make this world a more awesome place together.

You're One-of-a-Kind: Don't forget, it's okay to be different. Actually, it's more than okay – it's awesome! Embrace your strengths, tackle problems like a champ, and chase after the things you love. That's the key to unlocking your inner greatness.

Getting Better Together: Remember how we talked about growing personally and being part of a strong team? Well, it's like teamwork makes the dream work. When you become a better you, it helps the whole gang around you grow, too. It's like a big circle of awesomeness.

Learning from Heroes: Those cool stories about heroes from the past and the ones we look up to today? They're not just stories. They're lessons. Learn from them – how they faced tough times, stayed smart, and made the world better. You can do some of that, too.

Finding Your Way: Being yourself is like a journey, not a destination. It's cool to try new things, make mistakes, and learn from them. J.K. Rowling had her share of struggles, but look at her now! Keep going, and you might discover something awesome about yourself.

Sticking Together: Remember how we said unity is like a superpower? Well, it's true. When people come together for good things, amazing stuff happens. Look at history – people standing up for what's right, working together to make the world a better place.

Using the Good Stuff in Real Life: Okay, here's the deal – all this cool stuff we've talked about isn't just for the books. It's for your life! Use these lessons to make your days better. Be kind, try new things, learn from your mistakes, and help others. That's how you sprinkle some of this goodness in your world.

So, as we wrap this up, remember that being great is something you carry inside you every day. It's not a secret club; it's for everyone. Use what you've learned to make your life and the world around you awesome. Each of us is like a special ingredient in a big recipe called life, and together, we make something beautiful. So go ahead, take away the good stuff and spread that positivity everywhere you go!

www.ingramcontent.com/pod-product-compliance
Lightning Source LLC
Chambersburg PA
CBHW052101150726
48002CB00002B/980